The Solar System

The Sun

Núria Roca & Carol Isern
Rocio Bonilla

BARRON'S

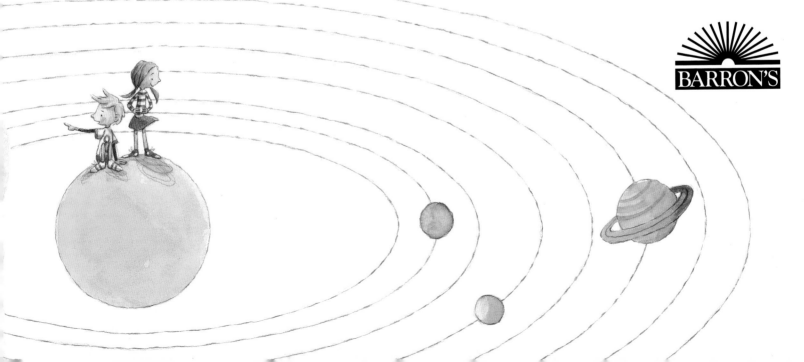

A sunny day

It's sunny today and Alice is happy because she can feel the Sun's heat. At last the clouds have gone and it has stopped raining. A dog is even stretching joyfully in the street because it is no longer cold.

But, Oliver is not so pleased because the heat of the Sun is melting the ice cream on his plate through the window!

A daytime star

The Sun provides heat because it is a star. And like all the other stars, the Sun is an enormous ball of gas that burns and burns endlessly.

Its temperature is so high that it heats and lights up the planets around it. "As if it were a gigantic oven!" says Oliver.

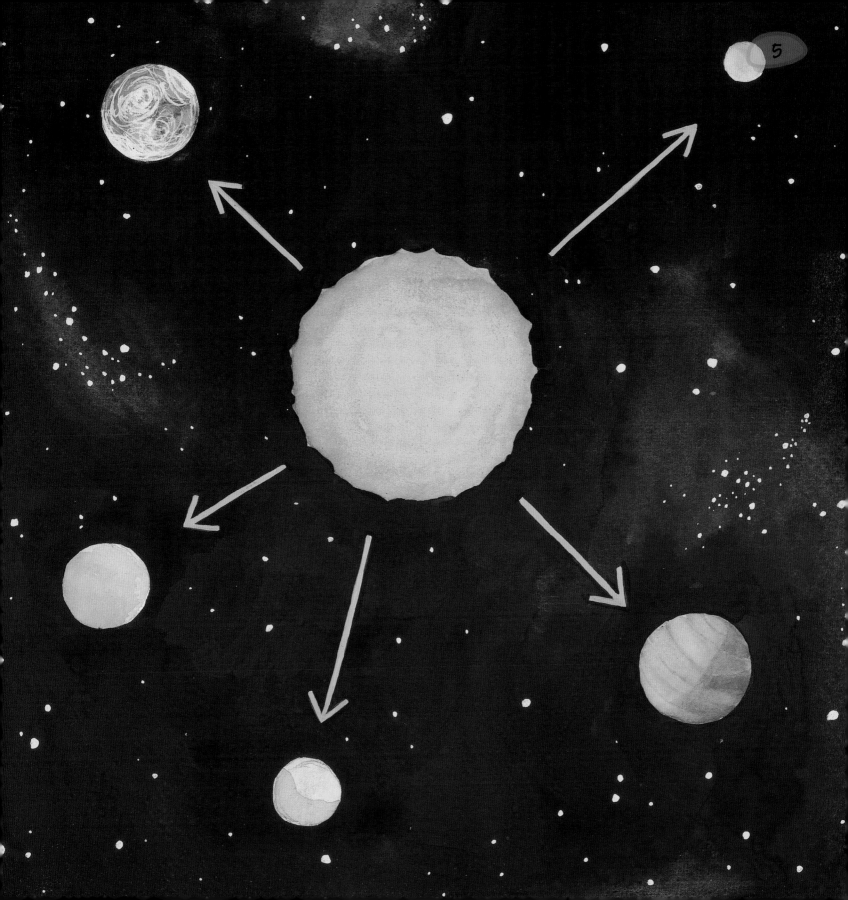

A planet full of life

Without the Sun, we would freeze on Earth because space is very cold—colder than in the freezer compartment in your fridge.

And without the Sun, no plants would be able to grow on Earth. "Then animals wouldn't have anything to eat!" says Oliver, alarmed.

Invisible solar rays

The Sun also tans us because it gives off ultraviolet rays, which are invisible rays that make your skin darker.

"The ultraviolet rays can harm us, which is why we should protect ourselves with sunscreen, hats, and sunglasses," warns Alice.

A gigantic sphere

The Sun is very large! It is so large that inside it, you could fit more than a thousand… more than 10,000… more than 100,000… more than ONE MILLION planets the size of the Earth!

If the Sun were a volleyball, beside it, the Earth would look like the head of a pin.

A sea of fire

Alice says that the place she would most like to visit in the universe is the Sun, but she knows that it's currently impossible to go there. The temperature is so high there that the spaceship would burn before arriving.

A long journey

The Sun is very far away! It's so far that if you wanted to go there by car, it would take... more than 1... more than 10... MORE THAN 100 YEARS!

But luckily, aerospace engineers continue researching so that we can travel faster and faster through space!

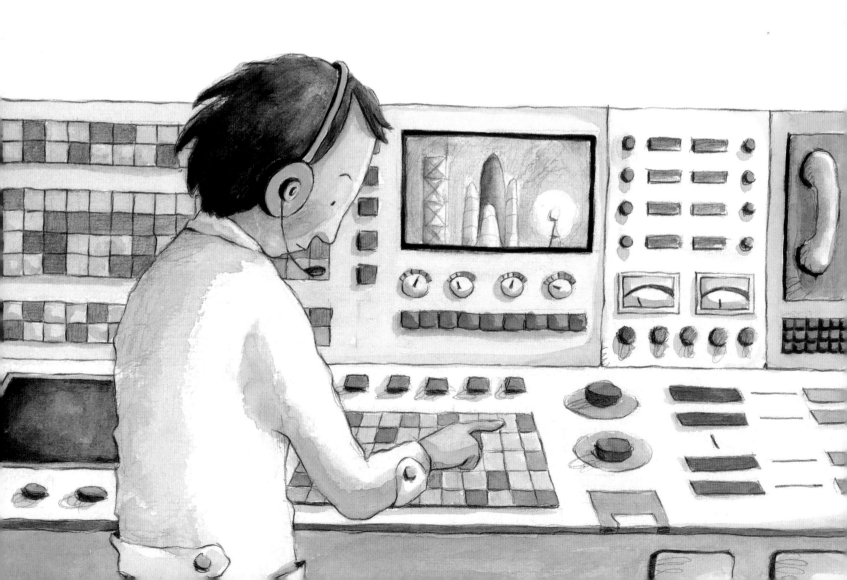

Traveling with light

Alice's mother, who is an astronomer, has explained to them that light is what travels the fastest in the whole universe.

Oliver imagined himself traveling on a ray of light... Then he would only take about 8 minutes to travel from the Sun to the Earth!

The center of the solar system

The Sun is in the center of the solar system. Very close to it, there is Mercury, small and red; behind it there is Venus; and then our planet, the Earth.

And beyond the Earth are the other planets of the solar
system: Mars, Jupiter, Saturn, Uranus, and Neptune.

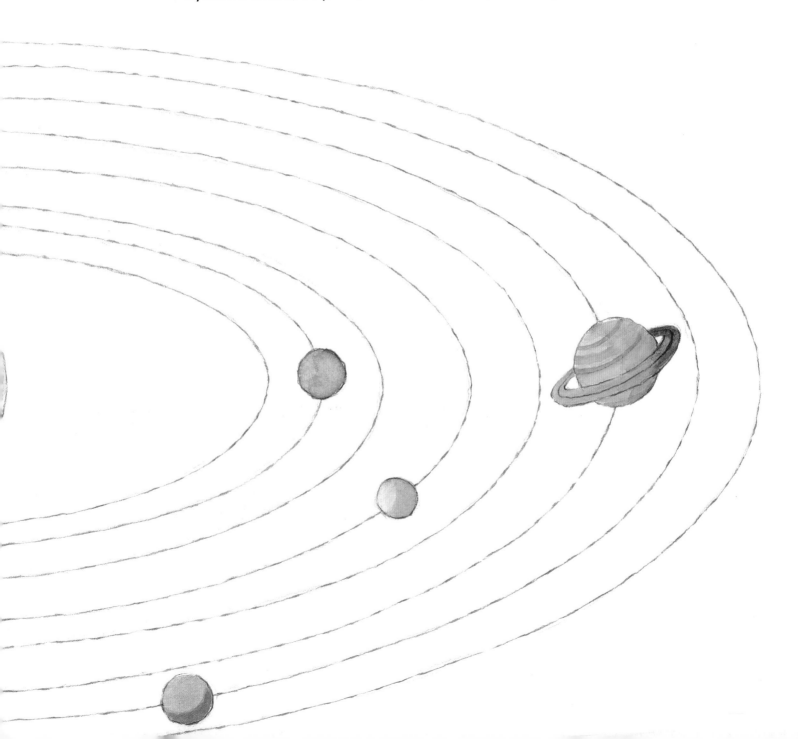

Distant suns

Our sun is not the only star in the universe: There are millions and millions of stars! You can see lots of them at night!

Some are much larger than our sun, but they are so far away that they are seen as tiny dots in the middle of the dark, night sky.

Asteroids

Lots of different sized rocks also travel through our solar system: Some could be the size of a small planet and others as small as a stone. All these pieces are called asteroids.

"Wow! Our solar system is full of things!" says Oliver.

Comets

Alice's mother has explained to them that sometimes we are also visited by pieces of rock and ice that come from much farther away than Neptune, the farthest planet in our solar system.

"These pieces of rock stuck to ice are called comets," says Alice.

The comets' tails

When comets enter our solar system, they start feeling heat from the Sun from very far away.

Then the ice starts to evaporate and the trail of gas and
dust left behind by the comet shines in the light of the Sun:
It looks like the comets have long tails!

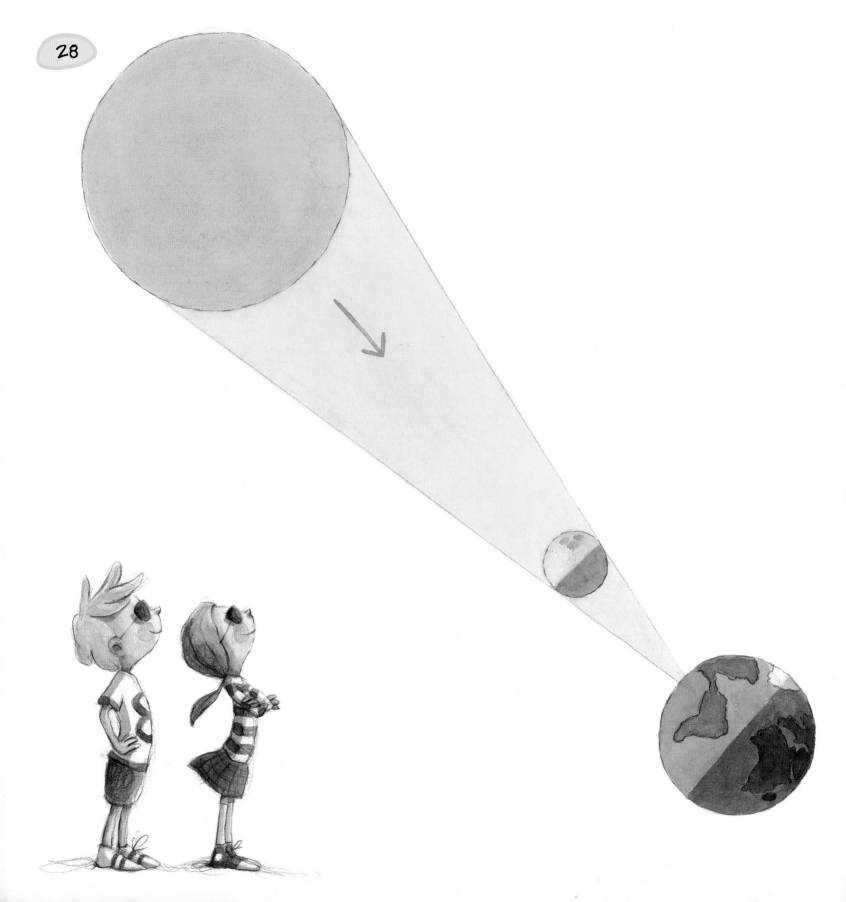

A solar eclipse

Today, Oliver and Alice are very exited. They are going to see a solar eclipse for the first time. You can't see that every day!

Looking at the Sun

Oliver and Alice know that it is very important not to look straight at the Sun. "Especially not with binoculars or with a telescope," says Oliver.

You need to protect your eyes to look at the Sun, because its light is very strong!

Activities

Draw the path of our star: A sundial

Ask a grown-up to help you gather materials to make your sundial. You will need a table outside, which could be in the playground or in your backyard. Stick a piece of poster board on the table with tape so that it doesn't fly away. Place a rod in the middle, which could be a pencil fixed with some modeling clay. Now, using a compass, note on the paper where north, south, east, and west are found. Now it's ready!

Early in the morning, draw the pencil's shadow on the poster board and at the tip of the shadow, note the time on the clock. You should do this every hour to observe the shadow that the Sun casts throughout the day. The next day, without the clock, you will know what time it is by looking at your sundial.

However, after a few days, you will realize that your sundial does not coincide exactly with your drawing. This happens because the path the Sun follows in the sky changes throughout the year: In summer it is closer to the south and in winter it is closer to the north!

Step on your shadow

You have probably seen your shadow on the ground many times. Shadows appear because rays of light always travel in a straight line until they encounter something they cannot pass through, like a tree, a house... or you! You can play by stepping on your shadow with your friends. One of you will be the chaser and the others must flee to avoid being stepped on. The chaser must go after the others and when he/she manages to step on one of their shadows, that person becomes the new chaser. If you play at different times of the day, you will see that the shadow is not always the same size: Sometimes it is longer and much taller than you, and other times it is so short that you can hardly see it. Then it's much harder to step on your friends' shadows!

The Sun is a star just like the ones we see in the night sky, but given that it is closer to us, we see it **larger and brighter**. We can explain to the children that in the daytime we don't see the stars because the Sun is so intense that it blocks out the rest of the lights. You can experiment with a lamp in full daylight on a sunny day. If you place it far away, you will observe that it is difficult to distinguish, as its light cannot be seen well. At night, on the other hand, the light is so intense that it can be seen from anywhere.

Parent's guide

Children tend to think that a very dense thing is always a solid, such as wood, but we should explain to them that a gas can also become compressed so much that it ends up being hard and dense like wood, while remaining a gas. All things, whether gases, liquids, or solids are made up of **"little balls" that we call atoms**, which are so tiny that we cannot see them.

Like our sun, the stars are large balls of gas inside which light and heat are formed. And they are the only astral bodies in the whole universe capable of doing so. The interior of the Sun consists of a gas made up of "little balls" of hydrogen that are joined together two by two to form other different "little balls," which are helium. When the little balls of hydrogen combine to form the little balls of helium, energy is released in the form of light and heat. **Inside the Sun, the temperature is 27,000,032°F (15,000,000°C).** By comparing it to an oven, which reaches 480°F (250°C) and burns a lot, you can get an idea about how hot it is in the center of the Sun.

A solar eclipse takes place when the Moon passes in front of the Sun, covering it from our view. During a solar eclipse, the light grows weak and the day darkens the more the Sun is covered. If the eclipse is total, you can manage to see the stars, although this only lasts for a few minutes. It is normal that some animals become agitated, that the birds fly to their nests, and that some dogs start barking.

Throughout the year, there are **at least two solar eclipses**, but you have to be in the right place for the few minutes that they last in order to see them.

Above all, you must remind the children **to protect their eyes** at all times:
• Never look directly at the Sun
• Don't look directly at the Sun with dark glasses or smoked glass
• You shouldn't look at it through glasses, binoculars, telescopes, or other devices that magnify images either
• Don't look at it through the camera viewer

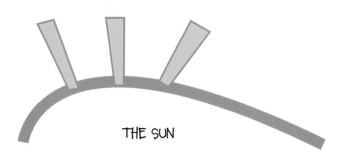

THE SUN

First edition for
North America published in 2014
by Barron's Educational Series, Inc.
© Gemser Publications, S.L. 2013
El Castell, 38 08329 Teià (Barcelona, Spain)
www.mercedesros.com
Text: Núria Roca and Carol Isern
Illustration: Rocio Bonilla
Design and layout: Estudi Guasch, S.L.

All inquiries should be addressed to:
Barron's Educational Series, Inc.
250 Wireless Boulevard
Hauppauge, NY 11788
www.barronseduc.com

ISBN: 978-1-4380-0478-5
Library of Congress Control Number: 2014935198

Date of Manufacture: June 2014
Manufactured by: L. Rex Printing Company Limited,
Dongguan City, Guangdong, China

Printed in China
9 8 7 6 5 4 3 2 1